Dr. Aruna Polisetty & Santosh Dora

Copyright © 2018 Dr. Aruna Polisetty

All rights reserved.

ISBN: 9781728603810

Captain Yoga

DEDICATED

To all with an endless spirit of Entrepreneurship

Dr. Aruna Polisetty & Santosh Dora

# CAPTAIN
# YOGA

Yogic Approach To Strategic Management & Leadership

Author

Dr. Aruna Polisetty & Santosh Dora

Edited by

Dr. N Bindu Madhavi

Captain Yoga

Dr. Aruna Polisetty & Santosh Dora

## CONTENTS

**Introduction**   7

1. Yoga: The Complete Taxonomy Strength and Wisdom   10

**Unit I  The Rationale: Sankhya**

2. Knowing the Rationale of Context: Samkhya   20
3. Evidence   26
4. Critical Evaluation   31
5. The Art & Science of Destruction and Construction   35
6. Niyama & Yama   39

**Unit II  The Physicality: Preyas**

7. Accepting the Change   45
8. Alignment   51
9. Getting Rid of Noise   54
10. Fortitude: Building a Robust System   58
11. Scaling & Strategy Formulation   61
12. Karma Yoga   64

**Unit III  The Perspective: Sreyas**

13. The Leader and the Driver: Raj Yoga   70
14. The Focus Principle: Dhyana Yoga   74
15. Knowing with Certitude: Gyana Yoga   79
16. The Corporate Mentor: Bhakti Yoga   84
17. Deliverance   86
18. Conclusion: Mission, Values & Broadbanding   88

## Captain Yoga

Dr. Aruna Polisetty & Santosh Dora

# INTRODUCTION

Yoga is 360 degree integration of key elements and power centers required for high levels of efficiency and elevation. The word yoga or *integrity* has evolved from *integer*, meaning *whole* or *complete*. In this context, integrity is the inner sense of "wholeness". Though yogic philosophies and practices were envisaged in the solitary seclusion of forests by the ancient Indian seers thousands of years back, its relevance and practicality is becoming more and more important in the current competitive times than ever before.

Western school of thought and psychology which teach sophisticated theories of business, leadership and strategic management happens to be at very peripheral levels and no way comparable to the deeply discerned and validated principles of yogic traditions since ages. Sympathetic management both internal and at organizational levels is not only possible but easy when one understands the art and science of yoga. Yoga is popularly known as a contortionist art of stretching the ligaments, for many people yoga seems to help to staying strong and healthy. Thus yoga provides a holistic approach to overall health and well being. For few, Yoga is a system of increasing physical and mental awareness. Attention to things which are otherwise ignored takes place inside you. However, the word Yoga is a process of connecting to the diverse phases of one's personality. It practically deals with the evolution of the human psyche and its successful sustenance universally withstanding the test of time.

## Captain Yoga

Though, there are many myths woven around yoga portraying it as Hindu religious practices out of ignorance or other motives, the fact is, yoga has no kinship with any religious precepts or belief systems. It teaches to *question* and *evaluate* on the basis of good reasoning rather than adhering to the superfluous rigid dogmas. It encourages independent thought and creativity that's best suited to oneself in accordance with the mission. Yoga does not advocate for a single strict practice for

everyone and everything but suggests different ways to different people with different propensities and capabilities to reach their goals. And it is this simplicity and suppleness which makes Yoga universal in its appeal. It stands eternally tall by providing ample room for continuous improvements along the way.

In the modern times, challenges of a corporate leader has grown manifold. A leader is an impressive personality above knowledge and expertise. He is verily the captain of a Business and organization. A leader has to continuously reinvent himself due to changing circumstances. It is less about learning many strategies, formulas and their successful implementation, and more about clearly understanding the context in its entirety and choosing to act wisely.

This book is an effort to make every individual more adept and adequate in the journey of life and in its various aspects.

Dr. Aruna Polisetty & Santosh Dora

*"Yoga Is For All &*

*A Yogi Is An* **EFFICIENT** *Person."*

# Chapter 1.
# Yoga: The Complete Taxonomy of Strength & Wisdom

Nothing in this world can be achieved without strength and wisdom. Yoga explains the complete taxonomy of strength and wisdom. The real strength comes from right knowledge and practice. Yogic practices are aimed to develop strength both outer and inner, of body and mind. It makes one realize the oneness of both mind and body.

Unlike other philosophies which give utmost importance to knowledge and wisdom over physical strength, yoga does not ignore the physical. It rightly recognizes the depreciating qualities of the body. Knowledge once gained cannot dwindle but our bodies due to its physical nature tend to erode in its strength if not given right practices. And it is this strength of our gross bodies that holds our subtle body or mind to function peacefully without any distractions of bodily ailments. It is wisdom to take care of the body. A suffering body is a house of negative thinking. Similarly, as a leader of an organization, you not only have to take care of your own health but also the health of your people. Many leaders fail to understand this aspect and do put every mechanism, rules and pressure tactics of fear and urgency that squeezes the strength and enthusiasm of their employees. Unfortunately, this has become the culture in most of the corporate, and it works well. Yes, it works but from outside and in short-term.

Economics is important, but it is the people who happen to be the driving force, the soul and life force behind the successful operations of any organization. People of loose faith and weaksouls can hardly help a company pursue its growth objectives. The physical supports and affects the meta physical. Yogic exercises appreciate the strength of our bodies and mind as an entity by awakening the dormant consciousness levels required for better decision making in every walk of our life. Before we delve deeper into the physical and the mental perspective of yoga, a clear understanding of body, mind, intellect and consciousness is prerogative.

For simplicity's sake, we chose to classify them into just two broad categories, the *Tangible* and the *Intangible*.

## THE TANGIBLE

### *Body*

It's the gross or physical part of existence. All that can be perceived by our sensory faculties of audio, visual, smell or touch is Body or tangible matter including the tangible sensory faculties. Body is the very first thing that is perceived by the senses.

A Soul however supreme, pure and sublime, by itself is powerless and incapable of performing anything in the absence of body, intellect and mind. One needs to have the right physical strength of Matter or Body and creativity and direction of Mind and Intellect to achieve its purpose. As discussed earlier Absolute or standalone things in isolation are powerless and are of little use. We are nothing in the absence of any of these entities. It is the combined wholesomeness or yoga that creates activity and real life.

## THE INTANGIBLE

Mind, Intellect, Consciousness and Soul are intangible because they cannot be seen by our sensory faculties. They are the finer elements. We cannot see through a person into the mind, intellect or consciousness of a person just by looking or touching. The intangible cannot be perceived by the tangible.

*Mind - Emotion, Intelligence & Imagination*

*Emotions*
At *Emotional* level every one of us are born with identical minds, I may call it the *original Mind* just for the sake of easy comprehension. This original Mind tends to remain same till we die. It's a mind that is instinctive and emotive. It does not care about good, bad, morals, values, facts, cultural behavior or boundaries of time and space. It's innocent just like an animal or a child. This mind of ours is very expressive and likes to act freely.

All of us know how children behave. If a child feels angry he will slap and bite instantly and beyond all our good reasoning will cry loudly at the smallest thing of unhappiness. When happy, a baby giggles from belly without being bothered about any sophisticated social reservations of etiquettes and dignity. When a child sees his favorite toy in the next door, he tries to grab it and run away. He is least bothered about the morals of stealing or whatsoever, and this is how I was in my childhood. I was fond of color sketch pens, in fact still I am. I was around 4 or 5 years old when I visited my aunt's place. There, while playing I found some color sketch pens lying under the bed. It was little dark down there but out of the litter, purple and parrot color sketch pens got my attention. They always attract me a lot. Even though, I already had those color pens, I kept them in my pocket and came back home. My elder sisters who caught me playing with those new pens scolded and shamed me for this act of mine. They told its stealing which is very bad. That time, I could hardly understand the meaning of the so called word stealing or the logic behind it why it should be bad?? I was made to return it, I did so with a heavy heart and a long face. I was prompted to say sorry too to my aunt. And, I remember, it was the first time I was made to feel embarrassed in my life. And, almost all of us continue to be same, least does it matter how old or matured we are, but we feel the same way. We wish to possess a thing of beauty, a thing of passion for ourselves without any morals; want to hit right on face of a person when angry if had it not been for all our learned social behavior or the fear of law or a simple self-conscious embarrassment of creating a scene, we would be doing it every single time.

Our Original Mind acts and feels just as a child does all our life. At basic Mind level we all are same!! We as grownups pursue the natural cravings of our *original* childlike mind but in a more sophisticated and educated manner.

## *Intelligence*

The mind of a man in common is like a chatter box which keeps on talking and playing the audio-visual feeds one has come across throughout the day, past few days or happenings of the past in the form of memories. It keeps collecting and keeps playing the gathered intelligence or information indiscreetly and wildly. Often, Intelligence is mistaken for Intellect. Intelligence is the capacity of Mind to gather information consciously or subconsciously. It's also how quickly one grasps the inputs, for how long one can retain actively and how fast it can retrieve the data at times required. Mind and Intelligence doesn't discriminate but just keeps on gathering, storing and repeating the information by habit. Not only does it repeat but it distorts and exaggerates in weird combinations. It's simple, free, and wild. It's because of this very effortless and limitless nature of mind that a man is *resourceful, Creative & imaginative*.

## **Intellect**

We develop our intellect over a period of time by being and interacting with our family, school, society and surroundings. It is our cultured or *educated* Mind. And since it is cultured and educated it acts as a Boss and is sophisticated. It is a logical mind that questions, reasons, analyses, pauses, plans, guides and takes the final decisive call over our original Mind. The capacity to stop and think before acting is something that makes a man intellectually superior than animals. Without the virtue of Intellect, Mind will behave in an unruly and impulsive manner. The more we exercise our intellect as a check post over the whims of our free natured Mind, the more control we have over our actions, reactions and emotions. It's the Master Mind. The good thing about Mind is, it somehow listens and obeys its superior, the Intellectual Boss. A well trained and efficient Mind is an asset for our whole being. And the bad thing is, it needs its own space and offs; and cannot always be dictated by the boss otherwise there is a danger of it either getting depressed or rebellious.

It may sound intriguing but just as a word of caution, intellect by itself is neither good nor bad. Intent is more important than Intellect. Intellect and Intelligence without good intent can be detrimental. Just as a Ruler with a bad intent can ruin the whole community and country. Intellectuals with nasty intent are more dangerous than simple street thugs and felons because it's easy for them fool and mislead simple masses by whitewashing their insidious plans under the garb of seemingly intelligent talks and clever rhetoric. This is the reason why we see corruption and crimes at big levels are master minded by intelligent and so called intellectuals with underlying nefarious intentions. As a wise leader of modern corporate you need to learn to respect and regard simple people with good intent more than giving undue importance to shallow intellectuals and people who talk glibly but with double intent.

## *Consciousness*

Consciousness can be understood as Mindfulness or *Awareness*. A Mind without wakefulness won't be able to grasp adequate information quickly and active memory or retention will be short. As a result, information retrieval becomes a tough thing job because of absent mindedness. On the contrary, a conscious mind is mindful of itself and everything and every information it comes across.

Without the light of Consciousness or Awareness in the backdrop both intelligence and intellect though not blank would be blacked out. They won't be able see clearly. Things will be ambiguous and in a state of obscurity. Decisions taken without consciousness are often miscalculated and off targeted, and there is always a danger of hurting our own selves. It's like groping for something when the power is gone or throwing our limbs fiercely trying to fight someone in a dark room. There is no discernment without Consciousness and things will be in a state of dithers. In the light of optimum Consciousness alone, we are able to take better decisions by understanding the larger picture or situation in hand by being able to look over the overall scenario. It's key for our situational awareness.

This mindfulness is very important for mind governance as the mind dreams and drifts freely always indulging in either

self-talk or playing the memories without any definite objective which is not good. When Mind becomes conscious or aware it stops jabbering just as the subordinates in any office do when they sense their activities are being observed by the Boss. The mess will continue as long as the boss doesn't mind.
Although minding or being aware of the mess itself is sufficient and mostly there is no need for further action to silence the noise.

Once there is silence, Intellect gets its part of attention. A conscious mind is less cluttered. It is now easy for the Intellect Boss to get things done in the desired direction through its subordinates Mind and Body. This very principle is successfully applied in the outside world for controlling crimes against women and certain other petty crimes like pedestrian lootings etc. Surprisingly the crime rates were considerably down without the use of power, patrolling or stringent renewal of clauses in punishment Laws and with almost zero cost!! And how was it done?? Simply by lighting up the badly lit streets and dark corners of the city and putting a virtual eye, the CCTV cams!! This made the people with criminal intents aware that they are being observed. It did not turn them into good as it was a mere external application but at obvious physical levels crimes were curbed. This quick fix though genius and largely successful, little impact did it have on people with obsessive mental conditions far beyond normal or on those who were power drunk with confident backgrounds and abilities to twist the laws in their favors. Mind should be trained while there is time and while it can be. Consciousness witness through yogic practices and more of its applications will be discussed in the following chapters due to its vast significance in developing Emotional Intelligence and awareness at transcendental levels.

Body, Mind & Intellect is an integral part of our being and should not be thought of in isolation. They affect each other and they all together define us. Body and mind is same, but it is perceived differently due to limits of perception. A mind is a micro Body or I may say a body is gross visible Mind. If our Mind is unhealthy and ailing, our Mental and intellectual powers become weak and depreciated and that reflects in body too. It looks pale, weak and sick. We shrink and become restrictive in moving around happily. In good Physical health, we feel confident and elated mentally. At times when we feel low a good straight posture and wearing a deliberate fake smile on our face can instantly cheer up our mental status and attitude; we feel more confident. There are many instances of people who have cured themselves of deadly diseases like cancer by simply watching comic shows and simply being cheerful!! By understanding the relationship of body and mind we can be better masters our lives.

*"Our Whole Entity Is A Comprehensive Expression Through Body, Directed By The Conscious Intellect, And Powered By Life Force Of Soul."*

Dr. Aruna Polisetty & Santosh Dora

# SANKHYA- THE RATIONALE

## Chapter 2
## Knowing the Rationale of Context: Samkhya

*"The Most Important Lessons Lay Not In What I Needed To Learn, But In What I First Needed To Unlearn."*

***Jim Collins***

*S*amkhya is a rationalistic approach to knowing. The essence of Yoga can be understood, when one can get in to Samkhya Yoga. Since, the yogic methods fundamentally rely on the practical foundations of Samkhya Yoga, which gives sense of every level of our existence from subsistence stage to the true realization of the life and self.

Seer Kapila(6th to 7th centuryB.C.)is believed to be the founder of Samkhya darshan or philosophy. Also popularly known as Kapilasutra. "Samkhya has a very long history. The ancient Buddhist Aśvaghoṣa describes Arda Kalama, the teacher of the young Buddha (420 B.C.) as a follower of ancient Samkhya tradition. It is the very second chapter of Bhagvad Geeta where Sri Krishna chooses to dispel the ignorance of Arjun through Samkhya's rationalistic rhetoric.

It is a Knowledge (Epistemology) based on realism. It sees things as it is and does not confer attributes or meaning to things on the basis of popular assumptions and theories. For the practitioners of Samkhya yoga everything is just a provisional theory or hypothesis accepted as a guide to future research and rational examination. It does not deny but it does not accept either. It is an atheist approach. It proposes three means of gaining correct knowledge through

## *Perception,*
## *Inference And*
## *Valid Testimony.*

The above form the basis of Samkhya philosophy which we will discuss in detail in the later chapter.

Samkhya goes into the very roots of life and existence and sees it as a combination of two unique forces, *Prakriti and Purusha*. Prakriti is the body or the unconscious material aspect of energy (Sakti) in simplest terms, it is vibrant and outgoing; and it does not have intellect, insight or consciousness. Purusha is the conscious decision maker. Our actions are guided by this very intellect of the conscious ego(ahamkara) which continuously interacts with the world through the sense objects. These two forces govern the activity of the body, mind, feelings and emotions of ours.

Every *object or living entity* has its own defining *property* or *Guna*. It emanates a unique energy, feel or emotion according to its form, texture and activity. Samkhya broadly classifies these qualities in three

***Sattva***
***Rajas &***
***Tamas***

*Sattva* are the qualities of goodness, wisdom and positivity. *Rajas* happens to be the quality of activity which can be potentially good or bad, as it is driven by action, passion and impulsiveness rather by wisdom of intellect; and ignorant, destructive behavior is attributed to as *tamas*.

Every human being happens to have these three gunas in various degrees and proportions. If a person is good, it does not mean he is devoid of other two *gunas*. It simply means one of gunas, the quality of positivity is dominantly active than others. We as human beings constantly interact with other beings in the world and come across situations which can awaken the dormant gunas at some point of time.

A business leader has to deal and formulate policies on various human aspects, knowing these trigunas is a must for a business leader who is on the top of decision making body of a company.

## SETTING UP GOALS

The modern leadership and B-Schools invest extensively in knowing the goals and a relentless pursuit of them. No doubt, it is important to know the goals thoroughly for in the want of it, every action and objective strategy is going to fail. Goals will never define ways definitively but they work as the destination points which should be arrived ultimately. But the question is, which goals to pursue?? What goals are good goals and promise success and positivity? No single approach is suitable for every person, product and business. All rationale tactics in the business are done to build confidence before investing your time and money. For estimating the demand, no single test is there, that can give you an answer. Slightly, it's a combination of all available methods, including your strong gut feeling for it.

For finding potential demand for your business and services, it is advisable look at niche opportunities that exist in and around and get an idea of demand for that niche. Validating an idea about demand for product is important because it helps you to get a sense, whether your business has no demand or potential demand before spending a lot of time and money on it.

Goals should never be made in isolation. Feasibility assessment is an important aspect when it comes to leadership success which must mapped keeping the various contextual elements in the back drop.

## THE RATIONALE OF CONTEXTUAL WISDOM

Samkhya calls for seeing things in the light of context than prejudging them based on stereotyped opinions and learned impressions. Entrepreneurial actions need to be guided by inner Wisdom. People are complicate and situations a many. The leader
needs to consciously awaken the innate qualities of sattva, rajas or tamas to best deal with them. Wisdom, combined with right action is essential for a good leadership. This

will make you different, since it puts you in a confident position when confronted by many challenges. In modern business lingo it is called **PESTLE** analysis (political, Economic, Social, Technological, Legal, Environmental) **SWOT** analysis, an analysis of Strength, Weakness, Opportunities and Threats. Below contexts should be learnt and known thoroughly before one actually moves in action.

## *The Context of People*

Every situation, every person is different. A leader has to make policies and many a times has to confront with people of different propensities on daily basis. He will be undeterred only when he truly understands the triguna composition in individuals and appreciates its beauty and importance. A true leader is a zealous missionary whose actions are based on his wisdom of understanding people and their problems. An entrepreneur, who wants to lead the team of his organization, has to deal situations in a matured way. To set out to resolve all our differences and conflicts with deep faith that all life is one and connected. He is not only compassionate but tactful enough to deal with people according their nature. This allows him to descend from his ego to take care of everything and to become more efficient by delegating jobs to appropriate people.

## *The Context of Social Practices and Laws*

Before setting up the goals and mission its mandatory to know the context of social ethos and laws in place. These are powerful forces which cannot be ignored or assumed to be bended in own favor easily. Fair or unfair is a subjective term. A business flourishes only when its acceptable and goes through the practical norms of the place and people.

## The Context of Settings: Time & Locale

It is a wise thing to launch any idea at the right time and in the right geographical location which finds the support of talent, technology, resource and supplies in an economic advantage. Geographical locations which are prone to calamities, political and social unrest should be avoided at costs.

*"Growth In Higher Dimensions Of Consciousness Begins With Samkhya Which Helps In Bringing About An Inner Transformation, Opening Up A Whole New Dimension Of Inner Strengths And Outer Opportunities Before Setting Sails To Achievement Of The Larger Goals. "*

"UNLEARN..."

# CHAPTER 3
# EVIDENCE

There are 3 important check list a wise person should consider for reaching to knowledge or certitude according to Samkhya Yoga. These three methods are the most predominant ways of knowing. Let us explore each one of them.

Knowledge gained with the help of senses
> ***Pratyaksa Pramana*** (Obvious or Empirical evidences)
> ***Anuman Pramana*** (By Inference, fair guessing based on knowledge)
> ***Shabda Pramana*** (Word of Authority or an Expert)

*"The Senses Are Gate Ways To Intelligence. There Is Nothing In The Intelligence Which Did Not First Pass Through The Senses"*

*- Aristotle*

Knowledge gained through Direct Sense Perception with the assistance of the 5 sensory organs are **Vision, Sound, Smell, Taste and Touch.** Mind, the Sixth sense, is the parental sense that holds and nurtures other senses to gather knowledge.

The logic of Atheists is based on the methods of perceiving. Samkhy does not seek knowledge at first

instance but contacts pieces of information helpful to reach the right knowledge in a scientific way. Ideally, knowledge should be derived from unbiased observation, but any single human observation is susceptible to various versions and number of different interpretations. You see an event and you see another, and because of your previous experiences, inferences and current emotional status, you presume(Anumana). *Pratyaksaand Anumana* Pramana are helpful in receiving and understanding the legitimate knowledge through
*Sabda* Pramana. As mentioned earlier this process is also called a top down approach in receiving knowledge.

## PRATYAKSA PRAMANA

There must be at least some faint ground if not a solid one to start with, and this is the importance of Pratyaksha Pramana which gives traction to the possessing of realistic and hypothetical knowledge based on supposition to laymen and experts equally.

Perception is how we experience our environment in response to factors surrounding us in different degrees and forms at different times. While perceiving our surroundings, we go beyond the obvious objective data of information available to us as our perception is always affected by our values, needs, emotions etc. There are many presumptions that affect human perception of objects, self, and others. When perceiving the physical environment, we tend to fill in the gaps by anticipating and deducing from the available information. Stereotypes influence our behavior. Sticking to Stereotypes alone leads to self-fulfilling prophecies. Stereotypical thinking is perpetuated because of our tendency to pay selective attention to aspects of the environment and ignore information inconsistent with our belief system. Understanding the Sankhya process gives us vital clues to understanding human behavior.

*A manager, who is in a leading position, should not perceive the environment and its problems like a layman. He must learn to see things as it is every single time with a fresh eye, since time is a factor that is constantly changing and with time other factors change too.*

Though it is important for the leaders and managers to acquire formal education in a particular field that gives them knowledge of
 their core subjects but more importantly they should understand
*the science* behind the knowledge. This will help in getting to the core of the problem or achieving the goals through the best way possible.

***"Theoretical Knowledge, Supported By Empirical Evidences Comes Handy But Only As A First Step To Move On."***

## Anumana Pramana

### Dr. Aruna Polisetty & Santosh Dora

This is going beyond finding and accessing information and the ability to see the unseen dimension of it by bending the perception both inside and outside.

In this fast-moving world, one is constantly under pressure to act now!! rather than spending a decent time on reasoning things thoroughly and thinking about the true facts. The quickest is considered the Smartest which is a dumb thing to believe and act like one.

A good Inference is a thinking process with utmost awareness that we go through to get from a fact to a decision or action. Biased inferences without awareness leads to disasters sooner or later.
As a good leader you should always strive to find and access very possible bit of information, and only then make a fair guessing, judgments or conclusions.

Drawing conclusions based on the interpreted facts and our assumptions; developing beliefs based on these conclusions and taking actions that seem "right" because they are based on what we believe creates a vicious circle. Our beliefs have a big impact on how we select from reality, and can lead us to ignore the true facts altogether.
Your beliefs and experiences should be a step stone to reach the truth rather than allowing them to be a blocking stone to narrow your field of discernment.

# SABDA PRAMANA

Sabda, Word of Authority or word of an expert must be taken into consideration while taking important decisions to avoid errors or grave concussions later.

At times like today, when the operations depends largely on information, distribution of it within the organizations has become a challenge due to the massive amount of information with which employees need to apply. Knowledge workers must therefore know how to independently identify and find such information, and verify the legitimacy of the same. As a leader of the an organization it is your responsibility to create a scientific thought and pipeline in the system that is purely research based and less based on assumptions. It is good to be independently thinking but the word of an expert should always be considered.

*Relevance Judgement:* The Use of analogical reasoning to relevance judgment enables employees to address successfully personal and current market related issues. Analogical reasoning is a knowledge-based problem-solving process in which decision making bodies and individuals apply information from precedents to new situations. Relevance judgment has its roots in Samkhya as the process by which individuals decide whether or not should a precedent be applicable to the problem at hand. The non-repetitive nature of knowledge workers' job is a crucial ability to apply information to new and changing situations. You will learn more about it as we move to the next step **Critical Evaluation.**

# CHAPTER 4

### Dr. Aruna Polisetty & Santosh Dora
# CRITICAL EVALUATION

The wisdom of Yoga in the Bhagavad Gita is not contained to spiritual discourse alone but it contains many leadership lessons that are much more comprehensive and scientific than modern management and leadership theories. It deals with the very core of human life and psyche than dealing with the outer surface of issues. It is also fascinating to find that there is no leadership or management concepts which has its roots outside the revelations of Gita. Gita reveals the truth to the despondent warrior Arjuna by revealing the truth layer by layer in a systematic way; no way did Sri Krishna tried to preach or forcefully thrust down his teaching on to Arjuna. It was a discourse between the two.

The First chapter of Gita, Arjuna Vishada Yoga, is about listening and taking all the inputs before jumping to apply one's mental and analytical faculties to solve a problem. A great proven leader like Sri Krishna absolutely refrained from giving instant solutions and chose to listen attentively to Arjuna.

Similarly, a leader must try to understand the mission statement of an enterprise first as a fundamental ground for taking decisions on his current issues or objectives. He should explore all the factors that affect the business and available resources at all disciplines. Then he will be in a good position to critically analyzes the issues and come to a decision. Many decision making processes take place in a situation where the information is not precisely known.

Choosing the best out of the available alternatives is an art of a manager.

## KITE Technique for critical Evaluation

*Know How* (Experience, Proficiency)
*Investigation* (Examine, Explore, Research)
*Testing* (Trailing, Experimentation)
*Estimate* (Evaluate, Assess)

### Know how (Experience, Proficiency)

Experience is a great guide. Past experience, therefore, plays a vital role in decision-making. Experienced managers usually consider regularly without realizing it, that the things they have productively accomplished was because of their past experience. Their past slip ups guide them to reach a reliable future decisions. This kind of attitude helps in expected growth with their increasing experience and progress to the higher levels in the organization.

*"Experience Lends A Hand In Arriving At Good Judgment."*

### Investigation (Examine, Explore, Research)

One should be cautious while relating past experience to the present situations, merely out of blind reverence for the old. As a sole guide for future action, it can be dangerous too. As a leading person, you should be in a position to investigate the reasons for failure. The nature of problem may look same but the solution might have to vary due to varying reasons behind the similar looking issue. Examine carefully all the factors. Experience can be used as a basis for decision making.

## Testing (Trailing, Experimentation)

Trailing one of the alternatives and seeing how it goes is a usual way of choosing an alternative. This kind of experimentation is often used in scientific inquiry. It is frequently suggested that this method should be used quite often in management. Only by experimenting with various alternatives a manager can be sure about the best way, especially in view of the intangible factors involved in the decision process.

The experimental method is likely to be the most expensive of all methods, particularly where it involves a substantial amount of money and manpower. Moreover, even after carrying out an experiment, doubts may remain about its certainty and real nature. Therefore, this should be used only after considering other alternatives.

## Estimate (Evaluate, Assess)

One of the best techniques for selecting from available alternatives is evaluating and analyzing the process you have opted for. This approach means solving a problem by comprehending it first. It, therefore, calls for a search for relationships among the more crucial variables, constraints and premises that bear upon the goal sought.

It is the *pen-and-paper* approach to decision-making. The solution of a planning problem and making a decision about it involves dissecting the problem into its component parts and studying their various quantitative and qualitative aspects which we will see in the next chapter "The Art & Science of Deconstruction & Construction"

Compared with experimentation, study and analysis are likely to be far cheaper. Study and analysis may require time and volumes of paper but usually they cost much less than trying various alternatives.

Dr. Aruna Polisetty & Santosh Dora

# Chapter 5
# The Art & Science of Destruction and Construction

The art and science of management has presently reached to high levels of complexity due to sudden surge of technological advancement and its short shelf life of it. Consumer behavior patterns are no longer the same and due to vast scope of market opportunities and new disruptive players there is a constant shift in demands and supply chain.

Many theories, concepts and models of management have been developed to guide managers in many ways. Any theory is derived from inductive and deductive reasoning. A system of hypothesis, accepted philosophies and a set of rules and procedures assist managers to analyze and explain the underlying causes of a given business situation and predict the outcome of alternate courses of action. The significance of yoga is its scientific and logical approach. It emphasizes greatly on the importance of destruction for construction process. No construction is possible without some destruction

> *"A Great Construction Requires A Great Destruction."*

If you as a leader or a manager are looking for a great change then you cannot avoid a great deal of destruction in the system. At certain times you might need to disrupt the entire system at a pace that your inductive and deductive wisdom calls for. This destruction does not always mean destruction at physical but most of the time doing away with mental beliefs. *Inductive* logic builds up or develops arguments towards a conclusion while *Deduction* pulls you away from your opinions on based on your past experiences." Inductive logic is *learning from experience*. We often observe *patterns, resemblances,* and other kinds of *regularities* in our experiences. It is a construct method of reasoning.

*"We Use Inductive Reasoning So Frequently In Everyday Life That Its Nature Generally Goes Unnoticed."*(H. Kahane and N. Cavender, *Logic and Contemporary Rhetoric,* 1998)

Deductive reasoning is sometimes described as a "top-down" form of logic because of making an conscious effort towards it , while inductive reasoning is considered "bottom-up." due to its involuntary nature.

**Inductive reasoning** is a method of reasoning that moves from specific instances to a general, In yoga, it this *Deductive Reasoning* that is the destruction of your past learning given an equal importance, is considered by many modern management scholars to be the standard for scientific research.

In a deductive argument there is always the possibility of new premises. Yoga always insists on practices to accommodate awareness to unaware actions happening by default within mind and body. Thus, by application of deductive thinking, there is healthy containment of one's habit of instantaneous conclusions and going to a specific approach rather than applying a generic method to every similar problem.

On the other hand the knowledge of inductive inputs is important too as it does provide us with ideas as a matter of general ethos which is very, very important to know and the possibilities that may follow. Therefore, they expand our knowledge about thesubject in a way that is impossible to achieve otherwise

*Scientific Experiment And Most Creative Endeavors, After All, Begin With A "Maybe," "Probably" Or "What If?" Mode Of Thinking, And This Is The World Of Inductive Reasoning.*- Cline, Austin. "Deductive and Inductive Logic in Arguments." Thought Co, Jan. 9, 2018, thoughtco.com/deductive-and-inductive-arguments-249754.)

All humans think but few question before acting. This questioning and will to analyze comes from constant practice of yoga which stresses on awareness. Destruction of popular theories and logical arguments is the ability to think creatively. Destruction offers opportunity to construct and derive new information and ideas by Deconstruction, analysis. It's a Top down approach.

Collective effort and ideation has a great potential than an individual idea while making decisions. In bottom up approach many will come up with their hidden talents, observations, ideas, views. This approach considers all members interest. A wise leader is one who has mastered the art and science of Destruction and Construction and he will be in a solid state of decision making. Then decision making will be more constructive ultimately.

# Chapter 6
# Niyama and Yama: The Imperative of Do's & Don't

Knowledge (Jnana) or experiential realization does not come from practice of yoga methods alone. Yoga is in fact only for those who practice one's rightful duties. Without yoga as a means, true knowledge is not revealed. So it is said by the one of the great yogic teachers, Shankara 'Yoga is for the purpose of knowledge of truth'

*Yama and Niyama* are often called "the 10 Commandments of Yoga." Each one of these Five Don'ts (Yama) and Five Do's (Niyama) is a supporting, liberating Pillar of Yoga. Yama means self-restraint in the sense of self-mastery, or abstention, and consists of five elements. Another, implication of *Yama* is punishment or dire consequences following the wrongfully committed actions. *Niyama* means observances which a wise individual must practice. Here is the complete list of these ten Pillars as given in Yoga Sutras 2:30,32:

All of these practices intend to successfully bring out the innate powers of the human being and to transcend one's abilities to self-realization and liberation

### Captain Yoga

The way, Yama (Don'ts) and Niyama (Do's) are often called "the Ten Commandments of Yoga, similarly they are the ten Do's and Don'ts for managers in the organization worth practicing.

Consciousness or awareness is difficult to reached in the want of understanding the Do's and Don'ts by the manager. Along with knowledge and experience as a corporate manager, you need to practice Dharma (i.e. duties, responsibilities, rights, lawful conduct, and true way of living.)to reach the pinnacle of your job not only in your organization but a leader who is looked upon with trust and inspiration by the entire industry, nation and world.

## Do's- Niyamas

*"Leadership Is All About Action And Setting Examples, And Not About Position."*

**Inspire:** Always remember that your crew observes you, and you should be an icon for them to follow. Be sure that your speech, conduct and actions inspires and them.

### *Communicate*

- Good communication can make an average manager great. Take time to talk to the team members, when possible sit and work along with them.

- Communicate them the organizational objectives and the bigger picture,; make sure they understand their roles and responsibilities, and your expectations.
- Show them you care and you'll soon have a reliable and productive team.

***Delegate:*** Allow your team to take on responsibilities, and provide them with all the resources needed to perform with effectiveness. Delegating and decentralization of power and Authority, makes them more productive while performing their tasks. They should be clear with their roles; they should not have role ambiguity due to overlapping job responsibility of other or multiple instruction from above. Everyone wants to contribute to the company's success – your job is to provide and effective leadership to make that happen

**Be a Guide:** A mentor's role is to guide the team towards the goal. Get their inputs and advice and then give your suggestions if needed. Discuss if you are not convinced. Trust your employees and also surrender for the team's success without any ego issues. Avoid the idea of giving orders and expecting them to follow them dot by dot, that is the way of creating slaves in a company. Lead to create leaders and you will soon see wonders happening.

**Be Grateful:** create a healthy work atmosphere by being friendly to groups and individual to keep them going with their full potential and performance. Motivated groups and individuals will achieve better results faster than others, simply because they enjoy their jobs. Appreciating and recognizing their efforts instills a feeling of pride and enthusiasm which works wonders.

## *"Gratitude is the Best Attitude."*

## DON'TS- YAMAS

***Don't be Egoistic:*** Your success will come through the success of your team especially in difficult times. Do not force your staff to do a physically impossible task just because taking undue advantage of your power and position. Don't get angry on the team for everything just as a habit. Treat your employees in a good way. Understand their problems and act upon. Be friendly with them.

***Don't be Rigid:*** *Flexible* working arrangements help teams and individuals to work productively. Flexibility works in both ways, teams definitely appreciate having managers who are flexible. Even for managers Flexibility skills are required in their teams to handle at different types of situations.

***Don't be Afraid of Conflict:*** Since a good amount of time goes in addressing conflicts while managing the affairs, management is no place for conflict-avoiders. Settle the fights wisely. Conflicting situations is an indispensable part of a manager's job.

***Don't Threaten:*** Many workers face a lot of intimidation from the higher-ups as they struggle to make their way in the business world. While some negative enforcement is a typical business practice, there is a line that bosses should never cross. Don't threaten your team members it will lead to negative results

*Don't be Inconsistent in behavior*: People like and need predictability. Don't be inconsistent in your behavior. Don't show mood swings. People do not mind working with a person with clear and understandable personality even if he or she has a tough personality. Erratic behavior drives people crazy and they are always apprehensive to perform at their best. for example, a manager who is jolly and upbeat one day, and controlling and aggressive the other day is difficult to work with.

Captain Yoga

# PREYAAS- THE PHYSICALITY

Dr. Aruna Polisetty & Santosh Dora

# Chapter 7
# Accepting the Change

*"Change Happens And It Is A Necessary Natural Mechanism For Progressive Evolution."*

It is your responsibility as a manager to exhibit to the employees about change and its positive outcome so that employees accept change with enthusiasm. Show them the opportunities and ideas that are brought about by change and emphasize the importance of change. In business, mostly change means advancements in technology for quick and faster production at less cost. Usually, employees view change as something that is harmful to their position or organization.

Usually, change occurs when leaders, who have been thinking to explore the business entity and tries to make a change. People at the top level discuss and debate on a particular change and take decisions and announce a plans. Change is joyfully admissible if the people in organization are told about the reasons and the benefits of the initiatives instead of plain circulation of information as rules. Change is adopted unwillingly, results in a lot of resistance and reluctance. As soon as the leaders at the top level decide to change, they should move in a correct direction.

**Fix On Goals, Not On Objectives And Strategies**: Organization moves with the predetermined goals and sets the objectives accordingly. Due to factors outside the control of organization, firm may need to change their objectives periodically which may be change in their production activities, or processes. For this change, they need to change resources and the approach they currently use. It can be usage of materials, it may be mechanization of production, and it may be adoption of new technology. It can be anything. Choose the best objective and work on the strategies that employees need to reach due to change and make them understand to reach the goals and vision. For this you need to

- *Systematize* tasks, organize activities and arrange the right roles for the right people. Define Clear roles and responsibilities of team and inform in time.

- *Articulate With Minimal Necessary Details*: Change can be major or minor. Clearly articulate why the change is taking place, and it future benefits.

- *Tap Ideas From All The Levels:* once the change is informed and explained to the team, ask them for the valuable feedback, tap the ideas from different levels. Listen to their views. Putting legs in their shoes will definitely give you the pros and cons of the decision.

- **Establish Targets And Yardsticks** that measure outcome and clarify to ensure that the firm is moving in the right direction.
- **Acknowledge The Response:** Collecting feedback from the team is important but even more important is acknowledging that feedback is being taken care of. Recognizing their views is very important.
- **Be Transparent:** change can be scary, communicate the change clearly, show discipline and be transparent with your team. Inform them why you have not considered their views in the decision criteria, if accepted thank them in a general meeting or through a circular/notice for their valuable suggestion.
- **Train Team**: if at all the change in roles and responsibilities creates any role ambiguity, give them proper training, and Encourage *team work*.
- **Reward**: Though some people may not show resistance and accept whatever initiative you are taking. Understand, they are the people who either do not understand or have submitted themselves to their jobs with a servile attitude. They do not have any connection or sense of

ownership in their roles and responsibilities. It is even more important to take them in confidence.

Have a plan in place to publicly reward those that make the time and effort to embrace change with good understanding. Especially those that do it with a good attitude and get other team members on board. Keeping the team properly motivated will aid in adoption of the changes.

*There are ample reasons for an employee to defend change in the work place. When an organization is considering objectives and its successful execution, the systems, technological advancement, organizational settings , cost reduction, streamlining the process for efficient turn around, and much more may happen. Employees fear that their roles might be reduced to eliminate and hence staffs resist changes.*

Employee's negative outlook towards change is detrimental to the overall functioning of an organization. Few employees view change as a prerequisite for the organization and are positive in approaching the change. But many employees view as a complaint and have a negative impact on the organization.

The main reason for many employees reluctant to change is fear and panic due to disruption of their comfort zones. They feel present working conditions are safe and comfortable. They refuse to change. Employees are accustomed to the routine ways of doing work , so they do not wish to operate and experiment outside their comfort zone.

Second, many employees see it as a managements way to do something or the other just for the sake of it and failing to understand the significance behind it. Even they do feel it is not compulsory for organizational growth. They feel change as unnecessary and disruptive.

*Lack of Creativity:* Create an environment for creative endeavours so they do inculcate an habit of experimentation and out of the box thinking. This will help greatly in making them less rigid towards change. Their hesitancy to adapt hinders the growth and survival of the organization in a competitive economy.

Flexibility in job descriptions, inter departmental training sessions will enhance the productivity and healthy environment among various departments whether horizontally or vertically. When mindsets are ready to take up any challenge with joy and pride profits are bound to follow.

## They Understand The Meaning:

The importance of effectively communicating the change is that employees are the backbone of an organization. They dedicate their skills and family time for meeting the organization's vision. When their contribution is acknowledged they feel more valuable. And, valuable

## Captain Yoga

employees are the most important assets during tough times

*"The Biggest Benefit Of Accepting Change Is* **NEW OPPORTUNITIES."**

# CHAPTER 8
# ALIGNMENT

Consciousness, functions through three different but closely connected entities, the body, mind and intellect. Similarly, an Organization functions through *Mind & intellect* of

*Purpose* (Vision)
*Stratagem* (Strategies to reach to achieve Vision)
*Communication* (Empathetically comprehending the strategies)
and executed by the *Body* that is
Human *Resource*, assets and other tools.

Organizational achievement or excellence is possible only with structured organizational alignment. Organizational alignment is crucial because all the aspects have to align with Purpose (Vision).

*"True Success Of Any Organization Is Reaching Its Vision And Mission."*

Vision can be reached strategically by setting objectives. No one can reach vision overnight. So break the Vision into accessible goals that is objectives. Objective can be best implemented through proper communication.

## Captain Yoga

Aligning all dimensions is vital for realizing Vision effectively within best possible means. This involves ensuring the appropriateness and effectiveness of the core business processes and the organizational structure designed to manage this. It includes the governance mechanisms that empower management and ensures accountability, and the setting and monitoring of performance objectives (performance management).In our work with organizations, we have found that a vision is effective when it aligns multiple departments well.

For example you started your business to become the market leader, it is inherent that, you want to be on the top in terms sales and revenue. Slowly, you make a better positioning in the minds of the customers. However, several factors limit you from not earning optimum profits such as scarce resources, lack of demand for the products, current market leader's monopoly, customer expectations, overall world market situation, technology, capital requirement for expansion , availability of skilled workers etc.

Align business Vision with Performance System and reward system of the organization. Add your Vision with what you are expecting from the employees (job role) and direct relation with rewards. Employees must see the connection between their work and the Vision of the company. But, how do you ensure that your rewards and business strategy are aligned?

Alignments a process of ensuring all aspects of your organization are aligned with realization of its strategy, operationally (the businesses ability to deliver its 'mission') and strategically (the management of the business to achieve its vision).

***Performance to Reward*** – Operational Feasibility (realization of Job Roles)
*Reward to Vision* – (Recognition to achieving the Vision)
Reward has a key role to play in demonstrating organizations values, commitment to employees and the value it places on performance.

Vision should be in such a way that, it should be configured according to the changes that takes places in the external environment.

There can be technological changes, change in demand and supply, intense competition, and other influencing factors such as business cycles, political, cultural, and government. Due to which the nature, scope and role of an employee change. Along with that business strategies should also change. The nature and role of work keeps changing in business strategy and hence re-structuring and re-configuring certain aspects at the work place is necessary.

## "YOGA IS ALIGNMENT FOR EXCELLENCE."

# CHAPTER 9
# GETTING RID OF NOISE

There is no organization which does not have grievances and noises of discontent within. Noises does not necessarily mean loud and obvious voices of dissatisfactions and strikes in modern times. Lack of confidence and mental disturbances due to dissatisfactory work culture is a noisy state as well. Even the best managed organization is bound to face the problem of internal dissatisfaction and discontentment. The reason can be many. Unfortunately, the truth is no organization can avoid it completely, but all possible efforts should be taken to ensure smooth functioning. The present chapter focuses on getting rid of grievance and building confidence and trust in leadership.

Peace is the prerequisite before anyone can work towards the achievement of goals. And, peace is possible only when people pose their confidence in the leadership. One of the best ways to gain confidence of the employees is to be in constant touch with them and communicating about changes and redressal of grievances in an efficient way. To achieve harmony in workplace about the leader should be

> *Transparent:* Lack of transparency is the main reason behind lack of trust in the working environment. Transparent leadership is the key for promoting trust between leader and workforce.

The more transparent you are in communicating the plans and work, the greater your workforce will be in theirs. Hence, remain transparent as much as possible in your actions to get best results. It creates trust in working environment.

Be wise while disclosing the information, so that their confidence is fortified.

*Openness:* To build trust among the workforce, along with the transparency, one need to establish openness. Establish a two way communication system where the employees feel safe to communicate openly with an management without the fear of being misjudged or misunderstood. Openness creates unrestricted access not only to knowledge and information but connects the leadership with the workforce at core emotional level.

When the information and knowledge flows without blockages, it makes space for qualitative information to be shared This makes the workforce confident and they work as a formidable collective force capable achieving targets in a splendid way than you ever expect.

*Know the Core Strengths* of workforce and allocate the responsibilities accordingly. A leader needs to identify the core strengths of workforce, based on his past experiences and present collaborative sharing of quality information. Many a time, leaders do not clarify the roles and responsibilities of workforce after changes are already in place in the organization. This leads to inefficiency in productivity and wastage of time. Hence, work should be distributed according to skills and talents.

> *"Do Nor Judge The Fish By Its Inability To Climb a Tree."*

*Be Accountable:* Keep your words. When holding an employee accountable, know for sure if you are not accountable to their welfare will lead to bigger failure slowly and silently. Because, workforce will struggle to understand the new direction of the company and how they going to survive in the new environment. It creates a feeling of insecurity which leads to preparation for change of job without management's knowledge. Hence, don't throw the blame on workforce for the failure. Be an example. Take the accountability.

*Spend time* with employees to understand them. In general, many employees behave different when they are in a group and when they are face to face. To get the feedback or opinion from this kind of workforce, leader needs to speak with employees one on one.

*Be consistent*: Be consistent and reliable for the workforce for your staff. A leader is someone who inspires confidence in workforce by standing by their side. A leader should maintain consistency in behavior and integrity.

*And, This Stands True Even For Leaders' Own Personal Life Situation Where He Needs To Find Peace By Getting Rid Of The Noises Before He Steps Into As A Leader Of A Company.*

# Chapter 10
# Fortitude- Building a robust System

Physicality and physical fortitude is an essential part of Yoga. That is why yogic practices stress on achieving an utmost degree of control and strength of the physique. The system, staff and functioning assets all form the spine and core of an organization. Great vision goes in vain if the core is weak. Great tasks can be responsibly discharged when the staff and your assets are well maintained and sufficiently managed.

There is an interesting story in *Ramanyana* about the vanara King Bali which tells the importance of physical fortitude. Bali had a boon from Lord Brahma that whoever confronts him in a combat, half of his opponents strength will go to Vali. This made him invincible. One day in arrogance he challenged Hanuman, who was meditating, for a combat. Hanuman was very much reluctant but finally agreed. Lord Indra, knowing hanuman's physical fortitude requested him to go only with one tenth of his actual powers.

When Hanuman entered the arena, Bali started to feel very, very uncomfortable with the sudden surge of power in his body. His muscles started to ooze blood and he was almost on a verge of literally bursting. His body could not take it, and he fled away

This story tells how important fortitude is important to hold and manage great power. As a leader and manager you should take utmost care of your own physical health and the health of your staff.

## *Train the Culture*

Everyone knows the value of experience, but to ensure you transform experience into skills that can be passed on and shared throughout the organization? A culture within an organization that understands good health and physicality is the key for long term growth and financial well being. Methods adopted within processes will facilitate a culture of physical well being. An organization that has mastered learning and productivity without compromising on the physical, can use that strength to adapt and react to any challenge it faces.

## *Immunity*

Every problem presents a hidden opportunity. There are many examples of innovation and breakthroughs that have been discovered off the back of something that started out as a problem. Use a structured problem solving process to quickly cut through layers of complexity to get to the root cause and improve on it. The process of understanding the context gives the platform you need to develop new and innovate solutions. Problem solving goes hand in hand with a learning culture, to enable quick and decisive response to any challenge faced.

Talk to any successful entrepreneur, or any professional with a positive attitude, and you'll find one key trait in common: all of them have a unique mentality that allows them to handle challenges. Rather than seeing problems as burdensome forces of opposition, they see problems as opportunities to fortify their current weakness, to learn, grow, improve, or adjust in a way that leaves them better off than before the problem existed.

This simple mentality has many benefits. First, it reduces the burden of stress that usually accompanies any new problem--because the problem is viewed in a positive light, it's less intimidating. Second, it contextualizes the problem. Because the mind immediately starts thinking about the effects and potential responses to the problem, it can be broken down and analyzed easier. Third, it encourages growth--this mentality forces you to adapt and improve on a constantly recurring basis. Finally, it's self-perpetuating. Every problem you view or solve this way makes future problems easier to handle, forming a positive cycle of reinforcement.

Unfortunately, productivity is conceived at the cost of health and well being which hurts the entire system into negativity.

## "A Strong And Confident System Is Built When All The Physical Aspects Of The Organization Is Taken Care Of."

# Chapter 11
# Scaling and Strategy Formulation

## Application Of Successful Strategy

Effective strategy, has its place in every business. Strategies are the detailed plan of achieving your goals and aims. There are many ways of arriving at a strategy. It is actually an insightful thing, and mastering it needs to be deeply connected with things at different levels for any environment.

Success at business or management doesn't happen by accident; it requires careful thought and planning. A key component of business planning involves the development and implementation of specific success strategies, which should be part of a written business plan you create before starting your business. Successful business strategies include areas, such as marketing, minimizing expenses, receiving compensation and continuing your education.

Yoga helps achieving goals in the most practical and natural way possible. Strategies build on mere formulas or limited observation will wrong if the holistic picture is not clear.

## Change Management

Every change starts with an idea, a vision of what could happen to create a tangible benefit for an organization. But ideas are not enough. Change or creativity is the first thing need for transforming a vision into a reality.

Change is a natural phenomenon, and management is no exception to it. And we all experience it all the time, from changing systems and cultures to meet the requirements of strategy, to changing potential customers into repeat business. Then there are changes in the external environment in the political & economic landscape, technology and modes of competition. Yogic principles help.

Leaders navigate their way through the challenges that each situation presents. These have been tested and refined over hundreds of years by seers and sages who operated on ground guiding the kings and masses for better management.

## *People & Process Management*

Managers today are enamored of processes. It's easy to see why many modern organizations are functional and hierarchical; they suffer from isolated departments, poor coordination, and limited lateral communication. Often, tasks are fragmented and compartmentalized, and managers find it difficult to get things done. Those who are in the field of business research have faced similar problems, struggling to describe organizational functioning in other than static, highly aggregated terms. For real progress to be made, the "proverbial 'black box,' the firm, has to be uncapped and studied from within."

Processes provide a likely solution. In the broadest sense, they can be defined as collections of tasks and activities that together and only together transform inputs into outputs. Within organizations, these inputs and outputs can be as varied as materials, information, and people. Common examples of processes are new product development, order fulfillment, and customer service; less obvious but equally legitimate candidates are resource allocation and decision making.

Yoga is not meditation or physical practices alone as many may believe but it is a complete life style which leads to one's goals in a strategic way. Similarly, every business has a range of key activities it performs for its customers. The skills of the people who do the stuff that the processes knowledge they use are a key resources for all organizations. People working within effective processes sets the culture which is prime for organizations best prospects.

## Effective Coordination

We all understand the importance of good coordination, and can think of the negative effects of poor coordination. The challenge is getting bigger.

Effective Communication is a process whereby coordination between various individuals and activities is brought out by communication. Effective communication facilitates information and exchange of ideas which helps to achieve the common purpose. Coordination is facilitated by exchange of ideas and information and brings people together.

*"It Is Unison Of Activities Which Works Wonders."*

# Chapter 12
# Karma Yoga

Karma Sanyasa yoga or simply karma yoga is the yoga of action; Karma yoga is not only the path of dedicated work, but it is the path of dedication towards the universal principle of awareness to one's roles and responsibilities in relation to other factors playing their roles simultaneously. A karma yogi is performs his duties in a selfless manner(Nishkama Karma) renouncing the results of actions as a spiritual offering rather than hoarding the results for oneself.

*The fundamental premise of Karma Yoga is that one is entitled to only perform actions, but not necessarily to the fruits of those actions.*

The Gita teaches the doctrine of uttermost detachment. In Bhisma Parva of Mahabharata epic, comprising 745 verses. Philosophical concepts of Gita's are Ishvara (The Supreme Controller), Jiva (Living beings/the soul), Prakrti (Matter), Karma (Action) and Kala (Time). Bhagavad Gita proposed that true enlightenment comes from growing beyond identification with the temporal ego and self. According to Krishna, the root of all suffering and discord is the agitation of the mind caused by a selfish desire. The only way to douse the flame of desire is by simultaneously stilling the mind through self-discipline and engaging oneself in a higher form of activity.

## Dr. Aruna Polisetty & Santosh Dora

Karma is both action and the result of action. What we experience today is the result of our karma, good and bad created by our own actions. This chain of cause and effect that we ourselves have created can be snapped by karma yoga. Karma yoga does not promise to give immunity against one's good or bad deeds but this constant awareness and acceptance of karmic effect make one a more wise person. Understanding the philosophy of Karma yoga is simple but many times its gets complicated too. Karma is cause and effect that is bound to happen. No one can denounce karma by action or inaction, there is always a karmic effect in place. Whether one abides by his duties, goes against his duties or chooses to stay neutral, every decision will have its karmic effect. It is impossible to avoid it.

The whole philosophy of yoga is very rational and is based on the practicalities of life and one's worldly career. Yoga deals with karma in the subtlest ways. It treats Manas, Vacha and Karma, all three as Karma only. Manas is the constant brooding and thinking that goes in our heads; vacha is the action of speech and karma as the physical involvement into a task. So, one is constantly doing some karma all the time. Since, it's happening all the time, yoga suggests to channelize this karma towards larger goals with awareness that we as individuals are discharging as our rightful duties and seeing the results in a more rational way. This is a great principle indeed!! Because when one becomes successful at work, one tends to take the complete credit personally forgetting that there were many suitable and supportive factors in place along with one's own actions. Similarly, when one becomes a failure, one becomes completely dejected and depression.

Understanding Karma yoga and its practices has a similar role that lead an individual towards work and a fruitful life. This plays an important role towards practical aspects of positive psychology to improve one's lifestyle and career as a leader of an organization.. A karma-yogi employee displays five great characteristics which are,

a) Emphasis on discharging duties than on outcome
b) Realizing one's action in context to larger picture,
c) Facing reality with equanimity and gratitude
d) Striving for excellence
e) Regarding work as an offering to higher Self(Ishvarapranidhana).

As these dimensions fulfill the employees higher order and spiritual needs they will positively influence employees several job attitudes.

## *Gratitude*

Karma yoga teaches Gratitude towards others. With regard to Karma-Yoga, it is doing work with astuteness as a rationale; by knowing how to work, one can obtain the greatest results. Man works with various motives. Some people want to get fame, and they work for fame, money, power, etc. Bhagavad Gita insists that we must all work incessantly and with due gratitude. All work is by nature composed of good and evil. In essence, it is detachment from the result of work. If working like slaves results in selfishness

and attachment, working as master of our own mind gives rise to the bliss of non-attachment.

## *Failure*

Failures and disappointments is a part and parcel of a leaders life. It holds a great value in itself as an invaluable experience down the line but dealing with stress is easier said than done. Stress, the major factor predisposing depression and diseases can be reduced just by overcoming anxiety. Overcoming worry over past mistakes and expectations about future is easy if one truly understands the karma as explained in yoga. This can be applied to the field of performance management to create organizations that are more ethical, creative and uplifting for its members. A leader who practices Karma yoga is never anxious and fear failure.. When one has no fear of failure, one does his duties more confidently, more strongly and this naturally increases one's success prospects.

## *Reward*

Traditional performance management is by default too much concerned with results particularly those that are quantifiable.

Karma yoga focuses on input efforts and contribution, rather than outputs or outcomes. Establishing the right kind of input measures is more crucial for suggesting quality and creative inputs from the staff than goading them for end results which often pushes the energy towards negative side.

*"Failure Is Never Final If One Learns From It And Understands The Real Reasons Behind It. One Can Become Successful When One Has A Heart Of A Karma Yogi."*

Dr. Aruna Polisetty & Santosh Dora

# SHREYAS- THE PERSPECTIVE

# CHAPTER 13
# THE LEADER AND THE DRIVER-RAJA YOGA

Raja Yoga, the royal knowledge has a special significance in yoga due to both its *physical* and *spiritual* nature. Rāja yoga has also been expressed as "sahaj marg", "classical yoga", Sarvanga and "ashtanga yoga" Knowing this yoga makes a person the complete owner. Every leader must understand his position and duties in proportion the organization and beyond. Yoga calls truth as *avyayam;* which is enduring in the sense that once attained it cannot be lost or taken away. Nor is it can ever be superseded, exaggerated, undermined or made up. It is truly there as it is. A leader who understands this acts in a most appropriate way by keeping his personal prejudices aside. Raja yoga calls for Yama and Niyama before one truly understands it. A person of frail and impetuous nature cannot become a Raja yogi.

This whole universe is driven by an unmanifest force. And, all that is manifest behave according to it. The true knowledge of the supreme force is deluded due to wrong self centered *samskaras* or education which narrows down the larger universal perspective. This unmanifest Avyakta exists everything. Indeed, everything that is seen or manifest is a miniscule part of this unmanifest driver. Though it is unseen, but it is very, very powerful and drives the whole universe. There is no point in the universe where is driver is not. There is an intimate connection between the driver and the driven, for all relative existence exists within the Unmanifest.

The human mind is limitless. And, this limitlessness is creates problems to if it is not trained. It The more it is under your conscious control, the more joyful and balanced one's being will be; that is the secret of raja yoga. It is natural to get swayed away by outward things and information but one needs a trained mind to stop and think from universal perspective. This is possible only when goes into the deeper and the innermost recesses of one's own mind.

This begins with the physical practices to realize the union of mind with the body. As discussed earlier the mind is a finer body and there is no such difference between mind and body except for some reason we have been falsely educated to believe so They are one or I may say it is one, it is not two. That is the reason when we become sick, we become sick in our entirety and when we become joyful, we experience joy in entirety and not differently in body or mind. When the body(body and mind) is sufficiently understood and is in unison, only then one can understand the outer world and its problem better.

According to the Raja-Yogi, the external world is but the gross form of the internal, or subtle. We are driven both by body and mind, for the sake of understanding, and not by mind alone. By the practice of yoga, we realize the true nature of ourselves which always operates in unison irrespective of our beliefs. The misinformation of unnecessary dissection of body into body and mind is obliterated by the practice of yoga.

## The Driver

Raja yoga is knowing about the supreme driving force behind the living beings. A good leader is a raja yogi since he recognizes the need of people and is identified with the basic driving force behind the living beings. The basic driving force is universal. People do work for survival but for fame, recognition and freedom. This is

the reason many times we hear people in lower working force boasting about their positions and their relationships with their immediate superiors.

*Amanaska*, a Shivaite yogic literature of 12th century CE or earlier, is a dialogue between Vamadeva and deity Shiva. It explains why it

is called Raja yoga or Royal Union. It is called so because it enables the yogi to reach the qualities of an illustrious king within oneself, the supreme self. A Raja yogi is a practical yogi who is ever serene and has chosen to operate efficiently in the material world rather than withdrawing oneself from the troubles and turmoil of responsibilities. He does his duties joyfully and like a king.

Raja yoga is the highest form of practicing Karma yoga, Gyana yoga and Dhyana Yoga. We will discuss about them in the next chapters elaborately with respect to management of business.

*"A True Leader Understands The True Driver."*

# Chapter 14
# The Focus Principle- Dhyana Yoga

*Dhyana* Yoga is the practice of meditation. Meditating and focusing on a certain thing as a witness is Dhyana Yoga. Without dhyana or focus we are incapable of doing literally anything let alone discharging great responsibilities. Without focus we cannot even pick a paper. With focus alone we achieve preciseness. Dhyanam is focusing on only necessary things and cutting away all other deviations and actions which are not useful for the purpose of achieving one's goals. It is difficult to bring an ever wandering mind under control. It needs constant practice and mental grit.

A weak mind full of fear and jealous is unfit for the practice of dhyana yoga. One must have a steady mind and right perspective to look at issues in a dispassionate way to get the most appropriate solution.

In Gita, Sri Krishna the charioteer of Arjun explains symbolically our body is like a chariot, which is driven by five horses which are the senses; the horses have reins in their mouths, which are in the hands of a charioteer; a passenger is sitting at the back of the chariot. It must be as per the wish and instructions of the passenger that the charioteer should guide the horses in the proper direction. If the passenger is not able to assert himself when the chariot is moving on a wrong direction then it is a dangerous state of affair.

In this analogy, the chariot is the body, the horses are the five senses, the reins in the mouth of the horses is the mind, the charioteer is the intellect, and the passenger seated behind is the real entity residing in the body. The senses always seek pleasure or happiness of momentary nature when the mind (reins) does not exercise restraint on the senses. And then, the intellect (charioteer) submits to the swaying mind and mind to the trivialities of the senses.

Thus, the senses decide the direction.

## *"..The Stronger Will Always Pull The Weaker Towards It."*

It is just a matter of which is the stronger, and which is guided and influenced by who. A chariot or an organization will go nowhere when it is driven by the whims of many horses (diversified goals). It is therefore mandatory to achieve the unison of intellect, mind and senses towards a focussed single goal.

### *Knowledge*

The intellect becomes stronger with Knowledge (Gyana) of self. Similarly, a leader should have the knowledge of business affairs before he can exercise his control over his people working under him. If the subordinates sense the weakness of the leader in his knowledge then there is a danger of being misguided and misled.

Many times even a good leader with a good intent is led into destruction due the lack of knowledge. Therefore, every leader should spend time to gather relevant information himself not solely depending on the subordinates to have a better sense and context of things. We will discuss this in detail in Gyana Yoga, the yoga of Knowledge.

## *Practice*

Knowledge itself is not sufficient to bring the mind under control. One needs to practice focus and meditation. Focus is utmost awareness in a very specific direction for the purpose of a greater understanding and control. We all know this by our own experience that we cannot perform only through knowledge but have to dedicate ourselves practicing the application of the same over a period of time in order to achieve results.

*Practice makes one stronger..*

## *Necessary For Strength*

A loose mind is weak and feeble due to lack of focus on few things. A mind which dearly dwells on many things get nothing. Only a strong and focussed mind can bear results.

### Dr. Aruna Polisetty & Santosh Dora

Be it a business or an individual, one has to work single minded towards a single goal to realize it quickly.

## *Dual Edge Sword*

Focus is a great practice but is a dual edge Sword in a sense if one focuses on wrong issues then the downfall comes sooner than expected. Focus should be made with discretion and with a definite purpose. Focussing without awareness leads to passion and self-pity, justifications, entanglement and other negativities.

Therefore, focus on only on issues that are important and totally eliminate issues which bears no significance towards the goals.

### DOWNSIZE

Most of us are aware of this term *Down Sizing* while working in organizations as managers or employees. It is a scary word. But, downsizing is a necessary way of sustenance. One cannot take good care of too many things at once. So, cutting down on spending the resources is a primary way of doing it. Though it is used as a compulsive mechanism in companies to survive and keeping on the healthy side of finance, it is a much misunderstood term.

Downsizing makes everyone back to their basics. It makes everyone to engage on necessary tasks alone making the best use of resources. Also, to be prepared for the adverse times. It is indeed a great tool to do smart work and discerning well in advance. When one is ample with resources, one tends to spend his time, money and energy on things that are not so necessary. The optimum usage of resources and the best possibilities are generally hidden in good times.

If the importance of downsizing can be understood before we actually start working on something, then there is a lesser necessity of downsizing by hiring and firing the people and cutting down on their promised perks and benefits. A mental culture of downsizing should be inculcated for efficiency. Being from the animation and films background, I can say the economics of it is largely beneficial. Even before a movie goes into on ground production process the downsizing process begins. Editing or deleting the shots is done by drawing storyboard panels. Doing these little thumbnail sketches on paper a saves lot of production time and money.

*"Every Business, Management And Leadership Should Focus On Few Things Only Especially In The Beginning."*

# Chapter 15
# Knowing with Certitude- Gyana Yoga

Gyana or Gyanam is knowledge which comes with the realization or experience. The world recognizes and poses a great deal of confidence in a person who is an experienced one. Experiential knowledge is the true measure of a person's real competence and qualification. Experience is knowing with certitude and it is not just a piece of information. It is an ultimate thing; it is not at all a primary step as suggested by Blooms taxonomy chart. Blooms taxonomy has a major flaw as it starts with knowing, comprehending and ends at Evaluation and creation.

Yogic process starts with unlearning one's previous learnings and dogmas, and then evaluating the contextual subject with a fresh perspective to reach to a conclusive knowledge through creative application, only then one attains knowledge which is true to ones best intellectual faculties.

Yoga stresses on knowledge through seeking. One has to have a mind of a seeker and not a believer.

#### Captain Yoga

## *"Knowledge Is The Reward Of A Seeker Alone Which Not Only Does Make One Stronger But Divine."*

### SITUATIONAL AWARENESS

Modern management and leadership principles are based mostly on preconceived knowledge and strategy building but a good leader must always strive for knowledge of the situation in hand and work towards it. Situational awareness is very important while dealing with business matters. To master this kind of supreme situational awareness Avaita Vedanta has proposed the path of Jnana Yoga to attain true knowledge by behaviours and practice.

### BEHAVIORS

Every situation differs so does the solution to it. It consists of fourfold attitudes, or behavioural qualifications:

*Discrimination* (Nityānitya vastu viveka, or simply viveka. Experience and gut comes as a handy tool but the ability to differentiate is a conscious effort that many managers lack due to behavioural laziness, over confidence or just ignorance.

If an issue is simply taken as another similar problem without proper discrimination, then a weak and short term solution is decided and the same problem will crop up time and again which will prove to a waste of time and mental resources.

*Dispassion of fruits* (Ihāmutrārtha phala bhoga virāgaor simply viraga The dispassionate indifference (virāga) to the outcome is desirable to avoid decisions made on vested interests. This is knowing the karmic effects and discharging one's duties as a warrior who gives his hundred percent without any selfish motives but keeps the larger and long term good of the organization alone in consideration.

*Six virtues* (Śamādi atka sampattior simply satsampat)

*Śama is* mental equanimity. A leader should not be afraid of uncomfortable situations. If one becomes uncomfortable or insecure or dislikes such situations one cannot think of becoming a great leader. A leader should deal with the situations cheerfully with wisdom and not in the haste of fearfulness or immediate avoidance.

*Dama* means restraint. Dama is having a good control over one's sensory faculties by practicing constant will power and assertiveness over one's natural propensities. It helps in understanding the other side of things as well.

Dama and Uparati removes the blindness due to weak mind and egoistic behaviour by moving the consciousness to higher perspective.

*Titiksa is* forbearance. An impatient manager is a bad manager. Allow things to happen at a practical pace.

Projects done on the graveyard of people are no good. Be patient and inculcate healthy work environment for the overall health of the organization.

*Śraddhā*s having good deal of faith on your staff. One you assign and delegate have faith on their abilities. Do not have doubts or show unnecessary impatience. Following up the progress is good but over follow ups is definitely going to kill their interest and enthusiasm ruining the entire motto of the tasks. It's the job the leader to make leaders at every level. Pose enough faith and confidence in work force and allow them to take the ownership of the task.

Samādhāna is concentration of mind. The acquired knowledge is incomplete and useless to a person who lacks an established mind. An established stable mind is a result of focussed contemplation or Dhyana Yoga which we have already discussed in the previous chapter.

*Drive* is hunger and looking forward for more and better things. A leader is always driven by a purpose with a specific vision for the company . This drive is necessary to outperform in a competitive market.

PRACTICES *Jnanayoga* consists of three practices: sravana (hearing), manana (thinking) and nididhyasana (meditation). This three-step methodology is rooted in the teachings of chapter 4 of the Brihadaranyaka Upanishad:

*Sravana*

A leader has to listen. You have to listen to your mentors, experts and subordinates. Listening is the gateway to knowledge.

*Manana* refers to thinking on these discussions and contemplating over the various ideas based on svadhyaya and sravana.

*Nididhyāsana* is the realization. It is the conviction of the facts and information as truth. This is the ultimate state which is Knowledge.

*"Knowledge is* POWER.*"*Francis Bacon

# Chapter 16
# The corporate Mentor-Bhakti Yoga

Bhakti yoga is a whole chapter on dedication and devotion towards the highest entity in Bhagvad Gita. One may be an expert in one's own arena of affairs, but Bhakthi yoga teaches to recognize the importance of a mentor, to rever a role model for inspiration and counseling at times needed. Bhakthi yoga is an ultimate tool for erasing the boundaries of one's individual ego and self centered approach with limitations of one's own experiences.

## Source of Inspiration

The beauty of bhakti yoga is it is simple to understand by everyone And, everyone get an inspiration from someone which works wonders without one knowing it consciously. When one revers somebody, one tends to copy his lifestyle and life philosophy in his life. We as a personality are a persona of someone else's. Though, it does not suggest we lose our individuality and become an imitated piece of someone else's. Most of us as individuals need someone to look upon as a source of hope and inspiration for psychological build up to perform greater tasks. Bhakti yoga proves to be source of instantaneous source of energy and enthusiasm.

## Dr. Aruna Polisetty & Santosh Dora

We draw inspiration from our favorite celebrity, the most successful industrialist, investor or any other person of highest caliber from relevant field. A person who lacks an attitude of bhakti or towards an higher entity get struck in his own limitations.

### Story of Ekalavya

There is a fantastic story exemplifying bhakti yoga in the Hindu epic Mahabharata about Ekalavya. Elavya happened to be boy of tribal origin who wanted to learn archery. Guru Drona was the best known teacher of his times. Ekalaya approaches guru Drona requesting for his kind mentorship. But unfortunately, guru Drona happened to the mentor for princes exclusively under the orders of the king. So he had to but deny Eklavya's earnest request.But, guru Drona's denial didn't deter or stop Ekalavya's mission to become a great archer. He didn't curse the guru but understood his job limitations and continued to devote him. He made a mud statue of Drona and started practicing rigorously in front of mud statue.

Ultimately he became an ace archer who was equal to Drona's direct and best disciple Arjun. That is the power of bhakti yoga!!

## "Great Stories Are Great Gurus"

# Chapter 17
# Deliverance

Thinking of deliverance and making the strategies is the general principle of any leadership management, but in yogic culture deliverance is kept secondary and building up a good system is of utmost importance. According to yogic philosophies of karma yoga results are bound to follow actions. Yoga is not about taking the complete control over the circumstances but it is about taking care of systems that are in one's control. This scientific approach delivers without the danger to being too obsessed with results.

## *Results Follow Actions*

With this realistic approach one slowly and steadily keeps building on one's strength and capabilities rather than breaking oneself of some unrealistic feats which one is not capable of. Another danger of modern day results oriented leadership is it does not provide any scope for failure and creativity due to undue pressures of rigid predefined targets.

If one exercises one is bound to become strong, even if he does not want to; on the contrary if one thinks of becoming strong but ignores exercise one cannot become strong. Exercising rigorously in gyms in the morning alone and having a sedentary life for the rest of the day is a very bad idea; this can put undue pressure on the system. One has do many small, small changes in one's lifestyle

This is the reason, yoga is not constrained to physical postures alone(Kriya yoga) as the day starts but should continue throughout the day with holistic approach through karma yoga, gyana -dhyana yoga, bhakti yoga etc for a complete well being.

Yoga recognizes actions as a predominant force than the deliverance or results which is however bound to follow down the line.

Sadhguru Jaggi Vasudev says about meditation that one does not need to forcefully put oneself in meditative mode to achieve spiritual heights but one simply needs to take care of one's body and lifestyle, then a meditative state of mind is the outcome it. To get fruits, one need not meditate on fruits but bring together soil, water, plant and sun together. This in itself will take care of the fruit; too much meditation on fruits is needless and ignorance.

*"Be A Warrior When It Comes To Delivering On Your Ambitions. And A Saint When It Comes To Treating People With Respect, Modeling Generosity, And Showing Up With Outright Love."*
***Robin S. Sharma***

# Chapter 18
# Conclusion: Mission, Values and Broad banding

Corporate leadership is an extensive subject. It is one of the arenas which contributes to the making of powerful economies through the management of wealth and human resources over generations. When you are a leader or an owner of an innovative firm or property, then your values and your sense of broad banding with the market pace are what going to make a big difference to your trust status.

> *" The Kind Of Values A Person Holds Is The Soul And Character Of A Person; It Is More Intrinsic Than One's Personality Which Is Visible To Most.*
> **Values Make A Leader."**

One of the most effective attributes of a practicing yogi is self-awareness and mindfulness. Conscious leaders who act beyond self-interests and follow the practices that serve the world and humanity is in true sense should be the guiding spirit of any leader anywhere. Whether you are leading a team small or big, your life or business, yoga elevates you to discern the correlation between the nature of existence and industry. Delivering as a leader in the modern times in very fast paced market economies is an ultimate challenge which only the toughest can handle with efficiency and efficacy. Yogic culture serves to make natural leaders who can sail through rough waters with an undying courage and innate strength that can be shaken by nothing.

In short, below qualities do naturally happen within a person who practices yoga.

*Integrity*
*Astuteness & Wisdom*
*Rationalistic Mindset*
*Sense of Gratitude*
*Devotion and dedication*
*Vision*
*A Focused and Equanimous Mind*
*Ability To Think Creatively*

# And most importantly,
## EMPOWERING PEOPLE

## ABOUT THE AUTHORS

*DR. ARUNA POLISETTY* (Asst. Professor, **GITAM University**) is a **Ph.D.** in *Finance* and holds several high accolade journals to her credit. She lives on the east coast of South India in Visakhapatnam city. She has been training many young minds while working in KL University and has a sound knowledge of all the aspects of business. Her research interests include Business Development, Venture capital analysis, and Consumer Behavior.

She aims to write several more books and journals to help create and establish an environment of comprehensive growth which benefits everyone in the social context.

*SANTOSH DORA* (CCO, Bluebert Games) is an exceptionally versatile artist and Character Animator in the field of *Animation, Gaming & Film Design*. Being in the industry for more than 12 years and having worked on both National and Hollywood feature films, Santosh now dreams of contributing towards higher goals and achievements.

He believes there is a huge potential in any field provided one has enthusiasm and sufficient information along with professional expertise.

## Notes

Captain Yoga
## Notes

## Notes

Captain Yoga
# Notes

## Notes

Captain Yoga

# Notes

## Notes

## Notes

## Notes

Captain Yoga
# Notes

## Notes

**Captain Yoga**
# Notes

www.ingramcontent.com/pod-product-compliance
Lightning Source LLC
Chambersburg PA
CBHW031444210526
45464CB00005B/2327